The Universe Within
The Unseen

Finding Light in All That is Hidden

Kanika Negi

India | USA | UK

Copyright © Kanika Negi
All Rights Reserved.

This book has been self-published with all reasonable efforts taken to make the material error-free by the author. No part of this book shall be used, reproduced in any manner whatsoever without written permission from the author, except in the case of brief quotations embodied in critical articles and reviews.

The Author of this book is solely responsible and liable for its content including but not limited to the views, representations, descriptions, statements, information, opinions, and references ["Content"]. The Content of this book shall not constitute or be construed or deemed to reflect the opinion or expression of the Publisher or Editor. Neither the Publisher nor Editor endorse or approve the Content of this book or guarantee the reliability, accuracy, or completeness of the Content published herein and do not make any representations or warranties of any kind, express or implied, including but not limited to the implied warranties of merchantability, fitness for a particular purpose.

The Publisher and Editor shall not be liable whatsoever...

Made with ❤ on the BookLeaf Publishing Platform
www.bookleafpub.in
www.bookleafpub.com

Dedication

*To my family and friends who have inspired me
to never give up.
To my heart, brave enough to embrace both pain
& renewal.
To my emotions, hope, and the human spirit.
To the innocence that lives within us all.
This book is dedicated to all those dreamers who
sees the universe within.*

Preface

This book holds years of emotions that often go unseen. We've all felt them; somewhere between growing up, gazing at the sky, somewhere between love and loss, grief and strength. These are not just poems. They are glimpses through the lens of someone who defines herself as chaotic. They reflect my emotions and inner universe constantly shifting, always alive. Each line is a piece of something I'm still trying to understand. A collection of moments that were left unsaid.

I hope you find something here that speaks to you.

Thank you for reading.
— Kanika Negi
With a way of living gracefully
September 2025

Acknowledgements

To those who stood beside me in my quietest days—*Thank you!!*
To those who never let my sparkle go away, reminded me that my voice mattered, especially when I couldn't believe it myself.
To everyone who found themselves between the lines of these poems—whether through memory, love, loss, or longing—*this book carries echoes of you.*
And to *BookLeaf Publishing,*
thank you for not only motivating me but for offering a space where my words could be seen & finally be heard.

1. Part I - "In The Bloom Of Time"

Before chaos claimed the world,
Did you pause to see the unfurled?
Of petals delicate, a gentle bloom,
A fragile grace in gentle room.

We search for the flaw in all we see,
And rarely notice life's quiet sheen.
The effort it takes to be the one,
Only to be plucked, and forever alone.

In anatomy, we learn of the butterfly effect,
But forget the years the soul must stretch.
What sacrifice, what pain endured,
To pierce the darkness, and radiance ensured.

How much pain does it take to be reborn,
To see the first light in this dark world?
A journey born of struggle and strife,
To find beauty in this fragile life.

2. The Universe Through a Child's Eyes

The mountain stood tall, where the sun liked to rise,
A river would just around a corner, near home, under skies.
When we were children, we'd draw all these things,
Not knowing one day, we called it peace.

The sky was a canvas, we make it colourful,
And stars in our pockets felt perfectly true.
The clouds became animals, dragons, and sheep,
We asked so many questions. No phone, just comics before sleep.

But now, all feels heavy; no more magic tales, no signs,

Just ceilings that sag with the weight of deadlines.

We weren't good or bad we were simply just **us,**
Floating and laughing without making any fuss.

The grown-ups would sail our boat with care,
But still found the time to smile when we'd stare.
They'd laugh at our jokes, we would admire them too big and tall.

I wonder how pure and beautiful it would be,
To see the whole world through a child's wide eyes.
It was never about some reward or a prize
It was just a game, through a child's eyes.

3. From The Roots

I never imagined the pain she bore,
Just to hold me in her arms once more.
The sleepless nights, the endless chores
No help, no pause, just random things, she is doing all alone.

Because that's what her mother taught her to be -
A strong woman, the eldest, a **tree.**

She stood tall, despite the strain,
With tired hands and silent pain.
Like roots beneath the earth unseen,
Her love held me upright, evergreen.

When I look into his eyes, I see
The weight of an invisible history.

Work. Eat. Sleep. Provide.
His childhood lost, nowhere to hide.

A boy turned man too soon, too fast,
Haunted by guilt from his own past.

We blamed him, sometimes we still do
For holding things we thought were due.
But he gave what he never had to give,
Taught by survival, not how to live.

It's not our fault, we grow from roots,
We take the sun, we bear the fruits.
But it's not their fault either, You see!
They were the first to be our tree.

And though the garden holds many the same,
Each root speaks with a different name.
In his silence, in her grace,
Are years of love we can't replace.

4. That One Lunchbox

Let's open the closet, feel the fun
The rainy dance, the morning sun
The fog from mouths in a quiet line
Childhood moments, frozen in time.

The bell would ring, We'd all assemble.
PT, music, art, and dance.
Our favorite kind of timetable.

Our backpacks weighed us down each day,
With math and maps and no delay.
But oh!! Those summers let us breathe,
Our only time to just believe.

Before deadlines and commitments,

Before savings accounts and grown-up limits,
Before skipping lunch
To hit the gym,
Before love, Before Netflix and chill!

There was just one thing
That truly mattered -

That one lunchbox.
We'd open it like a treasure chest,
Sit together like hungry wolves,
Tearing into every bite,
Sharing, giggling,
Roaming here and there.

Mistakes weren't scary
They were fun.
We wore friendship bands
Like we'd already won.

And yes!!
I still have those friends with me.
The closest galaxies to my heart.

I thank the universe every day
For giving me that time.
That table, that laughter,
That lunchbox,

We thought was just a meal,
But now, if I ever get a chance to take back.
I'd never miss that lunch break.

We didn't know it then,
But inside every lunchbox,
Inside every silly fight and friendship band—
Was a whole universe.

5. Youth in Motion

At first, it was a light game
I never thought they'd lead this way
We walked through days like laughter,
No burden, just some moments to spare.
The journey was simple, the road so clear,
No fear, no doubt, just joy everywhere.

But with each step we moved,
The path ahead began to be outgrown.
Life became deeper,
For every step asks more than we dare.

But today, in the here and the now,
We stand in youth, a promise somehow.
We chase the world but have nowhere to hide.
We rise with hope, we fall with grace,

Love and loss, the reckless race.
And in the cracks where dreams once lay,
Heartbreak whispers, stealing the way.

The first step was light, the second now heavy,
The road to the future both sharp and unsteady.
From laughter to tears, from love to pain,
Each step we take, we lose and gain.
So we stand at the edge, on the brink of it all,
Youth calls us forward, to rise, to fall.

6. Part - II "Wildfire Hearts"

We were wild & free,
Every rule was something to make us glee.
Something happened one night,
In the dark room, there was a dim light.

Someone saw us!

Freedom become fire,
We then come to know love wasn't kind or gentle.
It danced, burned, make us bleed,
Yet silent steps kept up the speed.

We didn't know what we were chasing,
Just our hearts were wildly racing.
Adrenaline rush, a flame so bright.
Like a wildfire, now we ride.

No one knows the way, but we all follow,
Like a flame that burns so bright and hollow.
It dances inside, a wild desire,
And we dance around its blazing fire.

No one knew, laughter turned to smiles,
Good mornings lost across the miles.
A wildfire burns deep in our veins,
We run the race with no known lanes.

7. The Ticking Time Bomb

Is this what pressure's meant to be?
It's not the way I pictured it.
A ticking time bomb under skin
No fuse, no flame, but built to win.

Be something, to become someone.
Study hard & shine like sun.
But every spark came with a cost
A part of youth, forever lost.

We stopped clapping on other's win,
As if their joy meant we had less.
No more jumping into life
Like we used to
careless, fearless, & feel light.

Still young, still soft, still full of doubt,
Yet forced to take a grown-up route.

No one told us growing up
Feels like being rushed into a room
With doors you're not allowed to open.
It is what it is! Keep moving.! Keep smiling.!

Like a ticking bomb,
we're wired to go
never stop, never afford to be slow.
Pretending we're not scared
We rise, we run, we risk it all.
Caught in life's relentless maze.
We wait to see what we've become.

8. Wrong Route

There was a moment
when life felt like life again.
When everything, somehow,
seemed to lead to this.

The first glance.
The first touch.
The first maybe.

A heartbeat
that didn't know how to slow down.
This was **love**
or something close to it.

The butterflies weren't quiet.

they kept asking for more,
like a never-ending road.

We were driving fast and low,
No sign ahead, no direction,
Just us!

We moved as long as the tank was full,
but eventually, we had to pull over.
Life! As it always does,
kept moving.

It was the first of everything:
the first time I felt it all.
And the first time,
Something was taken from me.

There's still an echo,
somewhere in the chest.
Not quite pain. Not quite joy.

Just that quiet ache
we call nostalgia.

9. Cut by Silence

Not every love ends with goodbye.
Some empty us from the inside
quietly, completely.

They break us
like glass, scattered across the floor.

A message never sent.
A silence too loud.
All we're left with
is the question, WHY?

I never thought silence could cut so deep.
I thought it was meant for peace
Instead, it created chaos inside me.

Now everything feels hollow,
emptied.
No crystal-clear reflection to see.
It's all broken.
Cut by silence, and it still hurts
every time someone touch it.

A pain without closure.
Some feel it fully.
Some born with blessing.

We blamed ourselves
for not being enough.
We blamed them
for being too much.

And after everything,
after all we gave,
we're still left

with the same word
burning in our mouths:

Why?

10. Burning House

You are finally home,
But while you were gone, it all burned down.
The walls remember the scream
Rising from my heart.

I turned the stove on
poured grease over myself
Not because I meant to,
But because I wanted
to be pure again.

You are home,
But it's all ashes now.
Can you smell the gas?
Everywhere you look
dark & empty.

The flowers once we planted are gone,
All left is fading memory

The home isn't home anymore,
Since you left.
Its just smoke & silence from the burning home.

11. Between Rain & Light

Ever wonder how rain falls with ease?
In youth, we taste love like a breeze.
We feel it deeply, pure and true,
But we also face the pain it can brew.
Like rain, it comes, then it goes,
Leaving behind memories, both high and low.

When it rains, we remember the ache,
The past comes flooding like a waking lake.
Moments we thought we left behind,
Rise again, replaying in our mind.
But as the storm fades, we start to see,
We, too, will find our way to be free.

For just as the rain will fade away,
So does the pain of love's dismay.

With time, the sharpness starts to wane,
And though rain may come, it's not the same strain.

Each storm of youth brings lessons new,
And every drop helps us break through.
Like rain, we don't stop; we rise and grow,
Through every trial, we learn to flow.

In the calm after, we rebuild,
With every phase, our hearts are filled.
The marks of the past fade, then blend,
Until we find peace and learn to mend.
One day, we'll look back and see
The rain came, but it set us free.

12. Part - III "Tending My Own Garden"

If truth be told,
I was never loved
because I never learned to love myself.

I watched the world
always giving, always kind,
like a flower, eager to offer its life
with no thought of return.

Someone gave me water,
someone placed me in the sun,
someone showcased my petals,
taking me out for fun.
I thought they admired me,
but all the while they forgot

it's the little things that matter most.
If only I had loved myself more,
maybe I would have bloomed differently.

So, I gave.
I gave everything, asked for nothing
just a glance of affection,
a smile that saw me as I am,
a heart that would cherish my beauty
and be happy to exist beside me.

If I had known the cost,
I would have turned away.
They came, wanting to plant me in their garden,
to mold me,
to tear my petals in a thousand pieces
and still they said, "You are the most beautiful
flower."

I wish I could love myself
the way I wanted to be loved.

But now, I've learned:
I am the flower,
not the bee.
And I will bloom for myself,
no longer needing anyone to see my worth.
I am tending my own garden now,
growing for myself,
in the quiet of my own light.

13. Where The Winds Whisper Changes

Something shifts in me!
The winds carry what I still hold on to.
I haven't learned to let things go,
But pain has shown it's okay not to know.

Like in youth, we believed in endless light,
But joy gave way to silent night.
Now as the winds begin to rise,
We're quieter under open skies.
A calm wind started to blow
We move like whispers, like a floating boat.

Was it always me, I think!
Or someone I've not known before?

A time will come, it comes for all
When our beliefs begin to fall.
We cross the river, slow and wide,
We bloom again, but not with pride.

We evolve in unknown ways,
Our roots reach deeper than before.
We stop clinging to battles,
We stop the fight, we become aware

We start to see, we start to feel,
That wounds don't break, they help!!
Its still confusing, gives us many emotions
The soul that once chased thrill and fire,
Now longs for peace not praise, not for desire.

14. People! Let Them....

Let people be different
in colour, in shade, in thought.
Let them make you wonder, not judge.
Some will scare you, others make you laugh.
Each one carries a face, a dream, or a desire to make you half.

Let them be confused!
Trying to fit in, they'll tie themselves in knots.
They'll work, eat, study, sleep on repeat,
Marching in rhythm & tired feet,
sleepless night, chasing goal through endless fight.

Let them wear masks.
Act strong

Let them hide their need for love,
All they do is shove them all.

Let them Grow up too fast.
Forget the muddy, carefree days.
Trade joy for glowing screens
and games that never end.

Let them the most intelligent,
the most capable, the most complex.
Let them to be proud,
let them become the monster they were afraid off.

Let them learn that in love, in kindness,
in simply being,
you might find the only path worth walking.

Let people be,

and maybe, just maybe,
they'll remember who they really are.

15. Black Swan, White Wings

She heard once that writing clears the mind,
brings peace, leaves the chaos behind.
But as she write, she start to doubt
Is this healing, or just a way out?

She is the Black Swan,
Not loud, not easy to figure out.
Grace in silence, too tired to care.
They thought patience meant permission,
Takes kindness for weakness.

Is she real, or some disguise?
A fading echo under borrowed skies.

They called her kind
Didn't seen her anger.
Even shadow forget who they are
When they stand darkness for long.

Now turning white, is a bliss
Not perfect but pure,
Letting her feel again.
All the smiles & good deeds along the way.

She's a warrior and wound in one,
The rising moon, the setting sun.
She's the storm and stillness, soft and strong
She has been both right and painfully wrong.

But even when she starts to break,
There's something here she will not fake,
She believes, love & kindness are the worth the risk.
She will be seen one day,
Not in shadow but in between

16. Where Stars Remember Love

Two lovers born from fate's thread,
One gave light, the other dread.
One healed heart with just a breath,
The other danced with dream of death.

Together forged through joy and pain,
One held calm, one fed the flame.

No need for flowers or grand display,
Only presence through the disarray.
Not in sun alone, but night as well.
In silent depths where shadows dwell.
They speak in the cloud, dances in rain.

A bond not built to chase or chain,
But held through fire, loss, and strain.
Both a question and a name.
Is it real, or fake?

They touched & cosmic broke.
The universe fell,
And the stars awoke.

No longer broken, lost, or small,
Rising steady after the fall.
Not seeking halves, but standing whole,
Not just a heart becoming soul.

Like a clear cloud, the stars glow.
Turning bright,
In the dark unseen.

17. Part IV - "Bird in the open sky"

We all were naive, now it's gone.
Time moves, phases passed,
Not kind, not rude,
Just cursed to touch the soul.

Like the bird in the open sky
We all just want to fly.

We made the cage, then blamed the hand.
That tired to set us free,
We held the key in our hand.
Now we fly high, fly away.

No fear for the future,

Just making beautiful today.

We fought the storm,
We all gave up once.
Now we look below through our broken wings,
We rise along the way.

The sky is vast and limitless.
No master guides this flight.
Our journey's different to write,
To ignite a heart or two.

Wings open now, ready, set, go !

18. The Child knocks

There is a soft knock, in the middle of silence.
A small hand reaches with wide, uncertain eyes.
There stands the child, a soul once tucked away
still pure, still whole, still fearing the world's
sharp edges.

A smile is given. A smile returns.
And something quiet begins to shift.
The memory stirs to laugh without reason,
to ask without fear, to dream beyond permission.

He wants the clouds, a house with horses,
and elephants too. Not out of logic,
but because the heart said so.

He dances, then sings, then laugh out loud
Not for applause, but because it feels good.
He doesn't care, what the world might say
only wants his friends to come out and play.

What will become of him, when the phase arrives.
the one we all must pass?
Will he vanish in the void, or rise & find?

His dreams are not too big,
not too small,
they simply are.

And now a quiet promise forms: a space will be made
where he is safe and free.
For HE is the hope, and must not be buried
beneath the noise of growing up.

Let him be. Let him stay.
Let him lead the way.

Because he is the flame, the fighter, the first truth.
And one day this universe, will be his dream come true.

19. To the universe within the unseen

To whom do I owe this apology?
For all I've carried along the way
Silent wars, yet never truly free,
Still, someone in this world cares for me.

No blame, no right, no wrong,
Just quiet thoughts, like a gentle song.
The sky may blur, yet I still burn the flame,
A light that flickers, yet remains the same.

I see the ache we all carry, Each thought, each pain,
Inside, we're all broken, waiting for touch says we're not alone.

We are all gardens, planted with care,
Not battlefields, nor made for despair.
We shine in our own, unique way.
It's okay to cry, to quit, to begin again today.

We are not trained with a map to follow,
No destination, no list to swallow.
We can leave at any time, if we choose,
If we shed the baggage, and refuse to lose.

The ones who stand with you are the ones that matter,
They see the universe inside you, like no other.
It's not unseen, it's not too far,
The colors of your soul, they shine like stars.

We pull, we push, like rubber bands tight,
We create a mess within, lost in the fight.

To whom do I owe this apology?

For the battles fought within me.

And yet, in all this mess,
I must see the universe within,
Each soil, each root, each blade of grass,
Defines my voice; my present, my past.

It's never too late, never too far
It's just the way we choose to see who we are.

www.ingramcontent.com/pod-product-compliance
Lightning Source LLC
Chambersburg PA
CBHW070500050426
42449CB00012B/3065